In Renaissance
Florence
with Leonardo

In Renaissance
Florence
with Leonardo

Text by Renzo Rossi
Illustrations by Alessandro Baldanzi

 **Marshall Cavendish**
Benchmark

New York

This edition first published in 2009 in North America by Marshall Cavendish Benchmark.

Marshall Cavendish Benchmark
99 White Plains Road
Tarrytown, NY 10591
www.marshallcavendish.us

Copyright © 2003 Italian edition, Andrea Dué s.r.l., Florence, Italy

Library of Congress Cataloging-in-Publication Data

Rossi, Renzo, 1940–
  In Renaissance Florence with Leonardo / by Renzo Rossi.
    p. cm.— (Come see my city)
  ISBN 978-0-7614-4329-2
  1. Leonardo, da Vinci, 1452–1519—Juvenile literature. 2. Renaissance—Italy—Florence—Juvenile literature. 3. Florence (Italy)—Social life and customs—Juvenile literature. I. Title.
  DG737.55.R67 2009
  945—dc22
                                    2008033038

Text: Renzo Rossi
Translation: Erika Pauli
Illustrations: Alessandro Baldanzi

Photographs: pp. 7, 16, 21, 42–43 Scala Archives, Florence

Printed in Malaysia
1 3 5 6 4 2

Contents

Our Guide:

Leonardo da Vinci

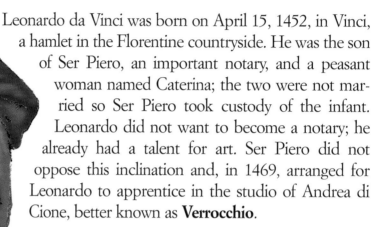

Leonardo da Vinci was born on April 15, 1452, in Vinci, a hamlet in the Florentine countryside. He was the son of Ser Piero, an important notary, and a peasant woman named Caterina; the two were not married so Ser Piero took custody of the infant. Leonardo did not want to become a notary; he already had a talent for art. Ser Piero did not oppose this inclination and, in 1469, arranged for Leonardo to apprentice in the studio of Andrea di Cione, better known as **Verrocchio**.

In addition to having natural talent, Leonardo was a quick learner. In 1475 he was allowed to paint the head of an angel and part of the landscape in Verrocchio's *Baptism of Christ*. Verrocchio, when he saw how perfect Leonardo's figure was and realized that his young pupil was outdoing him, purportedly broke his brush and declared he would give up painting. It was in this period that Leonardo painted some of his most famous pictures, including the ***Annunciation*** (1471–1474) that is now in the Uffizi Museum in Florence.

Above: Leonardo da Vinci was a very early pioneer in aviation. He studied the flight of birds and tried to construct a device that would enable men to fly. This wooden model of his flying machine, complete with a wooden man, is based on da Vinci's drawings.

As Verrocchio's best pupil, Leonardo was often a guest of **Lorenzo de' Medici** (Lorenzo the Magnificent) in the palace of Via Larga, where artists and scholars gathered. In 1482 Leonardo's life changed when Lorenzo recommended him to Ludovico il Moro, lord of Milan. Leonardo moved to Milan and was commissioned to cast a great equestrian statue dedicated to Francesco Sforza, the founder of the Milanese dynasty.

In Milan Leonardo painted masterpieces such as the *Virgin of the Rocks* (1483–1486) and the *Last Supper* (1495–1498), a fresco in the refectory of the convent of Santa Maria delle Grazie. Leonardo was not just a painter; he also designed a network of canals, studied human anatomy, and wrote treatises on light, motion, percussion, and weight. The statue of Sforza never got beyond the plaster model, which was destroyed in 1499 when Milanese territory was invaded by the troops of French king Louis XII.

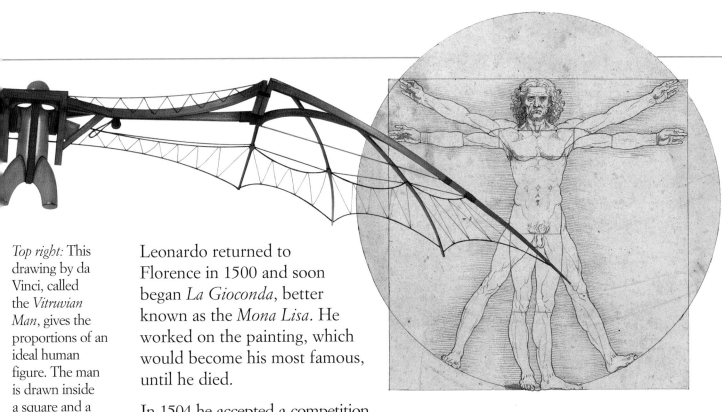

Top right: This drawing by da Vinci, called the *Vitruvian Man*, gives the proportions of an ideal human figure. The man is drawn inside a square and a circle to illustrate the symmetry.

Below: Patron of the arts Lorenzo de' Medici is surrounded by artists in this seventeenth-century fresco.

Leonardo returned to Florence in 1500 and soon began *La Gioconda*, better known as the *Mona Lisa*. He worked on the painting, which would become his most famous, until he died.

In 1504 he accepted a competition with **Michelangelo**. The artists were commissioned to paint two victorious episodes from Florentine military history for the new Council Hall in Palazzo Vecchio. Michelangelo was to paint the Battle of Cascina and Leonardo the Battle of Anghiari. Unfortunately, nothing remains of this competition except indirect evidence. Michelangelo got only as far as the sketches, which were subsequently lost. Leonardo tried a new technique and the colors melted, destroying the entire work. All we have are the preparatory drawings and a copy of the central scene by the Flemish painter Peter Paul Rubens (1577–1640).

In 1506 Leonardo left Florence for good, moving first to Milan and then to Rome, where the greatest artists of the time lived. In 1517 he accepted the invitation of the king of France, Francis I, and settled in the court residence near Amboise on the Loire River. He died there on May 2, 1519. It is said that Francis I came to Leonardo's bedside to pay the great artist his last respects.

Map of the City

The Florentines are proud of their city's history and have worked for centuries to preserve it. The city, which is the cradle of the Renaissance, is home to many architectural master-pieces; monuments and buildings honor events, artists, statesmen, and writers that shaped the city of Florence.

During the Renaissance, Florence was a symbol of civilization; all of Europe admired the city's art and culture. Florence succeeded in maintaining its status as a role model even during difficult times in history.

Bombing and fighting during World War II damaged much of the city's artistic heritage, as did a flood in 1966. Florence recovered with great courage thanks to the determination of the citizens and the support of the international community.

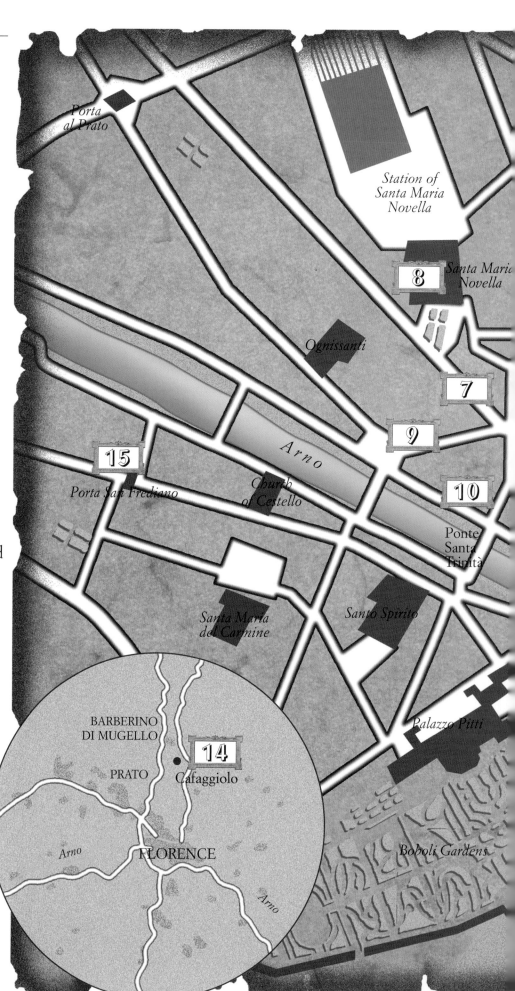

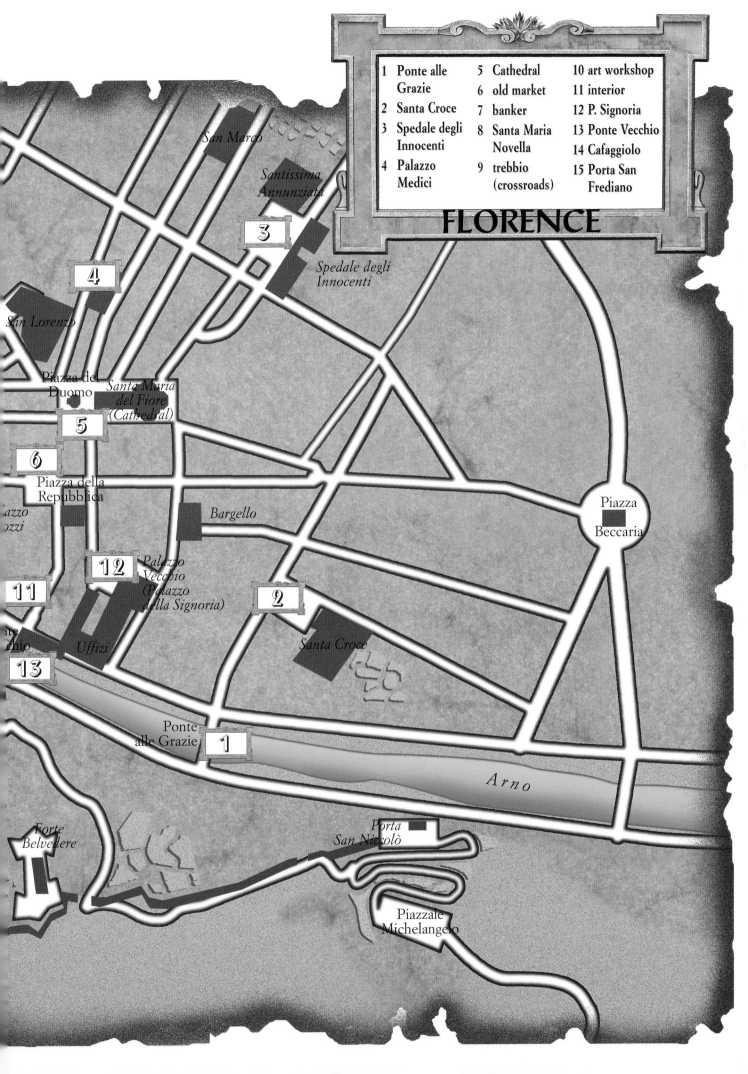

FLORENCE

1 Ponte alle Grazie
2 Santa Croce
3 Spedale degli Innocenti
4 Palazzo Medici
5 Cathedral
6 old market
7 banker
8 Santa Maria Novella
9 trebbio (crossroads)
10 art workshop
11 interior
12 P. Signoria
13 Ponte Vecchio
14 Cafaggiolo
15 Porta San Frediano

San Marco

Santissima Annunziata

Spedale degli Innocenti

San Lorenzo

Piazza del Duomo

Santa Maria del Fiore (Cathedral)

Piazza della Repubblica

Bargello

Palazzo Vecchio (Palazzo della Signoria)

Uffizi

Santa Croce

Piazza Beccaria

Ponte alle Grazie

Arno

Forte Belvedere

Porta San Niccolò

Piazzale Michelangelo

Florence!

Here I was, on the terrace of Piazza Michelangelo, with a breathtaking view of the city below. The orange roofs of the city stood out against the bright blue sky. The palazzo (grand buildings), bell towers, church domes, and bridges looked like paper cut-outs. "Florence! I'm in Florence!" I had to pinch myself to make sure I wasn't dreaming.

"Hi, I'm Andy," said the cute boy who had been sitting behind me on the tour bus. "How about walking down into the city for some ice cream?" he asked.

"Not a bad idea," I said smiling. "That way we could explore the city by ourselves. But I have to check with my parents first."

"In case you haven't noticed, our parents are sitting right over there having some

Ponte Vecchio   *Uffizi*   *Ponte alle Grazie*   *Palazzo Vecchio*

ice cream themselves. We've got a couple of hours to spend in the city and have lunch. I'd just as soon have a sandwich and not waste time in a restaurant."

It didn't take long to convince our parents to let us go off on our own. We started out along a tree-shaded boulevard that curved down toward the Arno River and the center of the city. Andy was studying his map of Florence to figure out where we should go.

"My name is Frannie, by the way," I said, a bit embarrassed.

"I know. I heard your mother call you."

In a few minutes we were at the Arno River crossing a bridge that the map said was Ponte alle Grazie.

Medici Chapels

Giotto's Bell Tower

Santa Maria del Fiore (cathedral)

Crossing the Bridge

From the middle of the Ponte alle Grazie we had a marvelous view of the Ponte Vecchio, a medieval bridge with three sturdy arches and a jumble of small houses built along its banks. The buildings were framed above by a long, uniform structure, sort of like a gallery or corridor.

"In my time it was different, but it's still beautiful and solid. A miracle of engineering, when you think it was built in 1345."

We turned around to see who had spoken. A rather handsome, middle-aged man with a beard and hair, which had once been a sort of copper color, was looking at us with kind eyes. He wore a full red cloak with white fur trim and a floppy purple velvet beret. Maybe they were filming a movie here, I thought.

"You said in your time—what do you mean? The Ponte Vecchio has been like this forever," said Andy suspiciously.

"No, my boy! When I left Florence in 1506 they hadn't built the corridor on top yet," the stranger replied. He didn't sound like an actor; he sounded crazy.

Andy, confused and maybe a bit fearful like me, muttered, "Okay, mister, we have to go now. We'd like to see the rest of the city."

"Wonderful! If you cross this bridge with me I'll be your guide to the Florence of 1504, a year that was very special, indeed."

I don't know why, but something told me he wasn't crazy and the idea of visiting the Florence of 1504 was exciting. Maybe he was serious. I hoped so.

"But that would be a miracle! And miracles like that don't happen to normal people like us," I said.

"Ah, but the great Leonardo can do everything."

"You're Leonardo?" we gasped, "Leonardo da Vinci, the painter?"

"Painter, architect, scientist, writer, musician, and mathematician. I'm also a master caster and a master mechanic, scenographer, and hydraulic engineer. In other words," he laughed, "I'm a genius!"

We didn't wait to have him repeat the invitation; we hurried across the bridge and plunged into the past.

The Triumph of the City

Crossing the Ponte alle Grazie was like stepping into a painting from the fifteenth century. The scene, atmosphere, and people all belonged to another era. People recognized Leonardo and greeted him respectfully or pointed him out to others who looked at him with reverence.

We found ourselves in a large, rectangular piazza; on every side were bleachers filled with noisy crowds. The piazza was decorated with brightly colored drapes and flags. At the back of the piazza was the bare façade of an imposing church.

"We're in Piazza Santa Croce, and that church is part of the Franciscan convent," explained Leonardo. "They began building it in 1228, the year **Francis of Assisi** was declared a saint. He's the one who talked to the birds and lived a life of poverty. The Franciscans, his followers, take vows of poverty. The church, which wasn't consecrated until 1442, was funded by wealthy Florentine families who wanted to be sure they would go to heaven. But the money ran out and the façade was never finished."

"That's the chapel of the **Pazzi** family and **Filippo Brunelleschi**, one of our greatest architects, designed it in 1430," said Leonardo as he pointed to the dome of a small structure next to the church. "It's a marvelous piece of work. Brunelleschi loved to play around with geometric shapes and the chapel is based on a module, a geometric form used as a measuring tool."

Just then, a procession of richly decorated wagons and a stream of people in costume entered the piazza.

"What's it all about?" I asked Leonardo, excitedly. "Is it some kind of celebration?"

"I'd say a public spectacle. It's called a triumph, a procession celebrating the city and those who govern it. Look, here's the float of Abundance, praising the wealth of Florence thanks to all its enterprising citizens, and the one after is the float of Temperance, a warning that wealth must be enjoyed with moderation."

"In other words, an educational pageant," declared Andy, "in an incredible setting."

THE PAZZI CHAPEL

The Pazzi family of Florence saw the Medici as adversaries and commissioned Filippo Brunelleschi to build a chapel. It was built between 1430 and 1445 and is one of the earliest examples of Renaissance architecture. The chapel is based on the harmony of circles and squares, which is particularly visible in the cupola and lantern. It is a gem of grace and elegance.

A Home for Orphans

We were swept along by the crowd leaving Piazza Santa Croce. Andy and I were disoriented and followed out guide closely, marveling at everything we passed. We arrived in another piazza, which was not nearly as chaotic. There was a church at one end and a building with an airy portico along thc side.

"This is the church dedicated to the Virgin of the Annunciation," explained Leonardo. "It's the most popular church in Florence with a miraculous painting of the Annunciation inside that is over three hundred years old. The Florentines are so devoted to Mary that their calendar begins the year on March 25, the day the Annunciation is celebrated."

"And that building over there?" I asked, recognizing it from one of my mother's art history textbooks.

"That's the Spedale degli Innocenti, or the orphanage that takes in abandoned babies. See over there where there's a sort of window? That's where mothers who can't keep their children leave them. There is a basin where she places the baby

Below: Andrea della Robbia made the roundels that adorn the Spedale degli Innocenti. People believed that tightly wrapping infants would make them straight and healthy.

and rings a bell so the nuns know to come and pick it up. You know this was one of the first of its kind in Europe. It was funded by the corporations—particularly the Silk **Guild**—and the richest families in the city.

There are women who nurse them, and they are taught to read and write and they learn a craft. Then when they are 14 or 15, the nuns find husbands for the girls and the boys go to work. Some even become very successful. It's not who you were born to that makes the man, but your will, your awareness of your dignity, and your knowledge. I should know!"

"Who built it?" asked Andy.

"Filippo Brunelleschi designed the portico, which was built between 1421 and 1434. If you know anything about ancient Greek architecture, you can see where he got his idea for the slender columns and the **Corinthian** capitals. Brunelleschi and the other artists of his school studied Greek architecture, which uses mathematical proportions. **Andrea della Robbia** added the glazed ceramic roundels between the arches."

As we came to a straight paved road that cut through the labyrinth of medieval lanes, Leonardo began to tell us more about his city: "Here we are in Via Larga, a sign of the new times and new culture in Florence. The street, like the surrounding district, was the territory of the Medicis, but the family was banished ten years ago. This palazzo was their official residence. Cosimo the Elder commissioned it from his friend **Michelozzo**, who worked on it from 1444 to 1459. Lorenzo de' Medici, Cosimo's grandson, established Via Larga as the cultural and political center of the city."

Andy had heard of the Medicis from his father, who was a history professor. He asked how many people lived in Florence in 1504.

"It's hard to say," Leonardo explained. "Don't forget that every so often we had epidemics of the **Black Death**—the plague—the most recent was only nine years ago. The worst one was in 1348 when at least one out of three died. If you count the 10,000 hearths, or families, in the suburbs, there should be about 80,000 inhabitants, but that doesn't include the monks, friars, and nuns. There seem to be more people joining religious orders every day! Of course the convents and monasteries do a lot of good work, like taking care of the sick and the poor."

"I guess convents are okay," said Andy doubtfully, "but Florence is famous for a lot of other things too. Like, maybe, ice cream?"

Leonardo paid no attention to him while I whispered that ice cream hadn't been invented in Leonardo's time.

"Just think," he continued, "more than 40 new palaces, both public and private, have been built in the last thirty years. There are about 20 hospitals, or shelters for travelers and the poor; 4 solid bridges over the Arno; 118 churches with cloisters, refectories, and libraries; and vast open spaces—approximately 50 squares, plus 30 *loggias* and 138 parks, gardens, and orchards."

"Wow, and are they all as impressive as what we've seen?" I asked.

"No, you're seeing only the best side. There are also gloomier places, like the Stinche, which is a foul-smelling prison, or the lanes next to it where cloth is dyed—Florence is famous for its woolen textiles, but the workers are practically slaves."

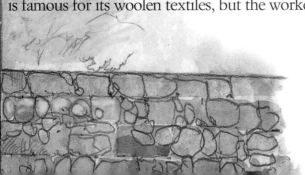

A Square Full of Treasures

A few steps from Via Larga and Palazzo Medici is the most precious treasure chest of Florence: Piazza del Duomo. Leonardo seemed impatient to begin the visit; his eyes shone with the pride of a Florentine and of an artist.

"There's no other place in the world where so many signs of human genius are to be found as in this square. The first signs of the rebirth of art are here: Brunelleschi's dome and **Ghiberti**'s doors. The Renaissance spread to other countries from here."

He led us to the center of the square and, with a sweep of his arm, indicated the cathedral with its imposing dome, **Giotto**'s 280-foot (85-m) bell tower, and the Baptistery of San Giovanni, or St. John.

5

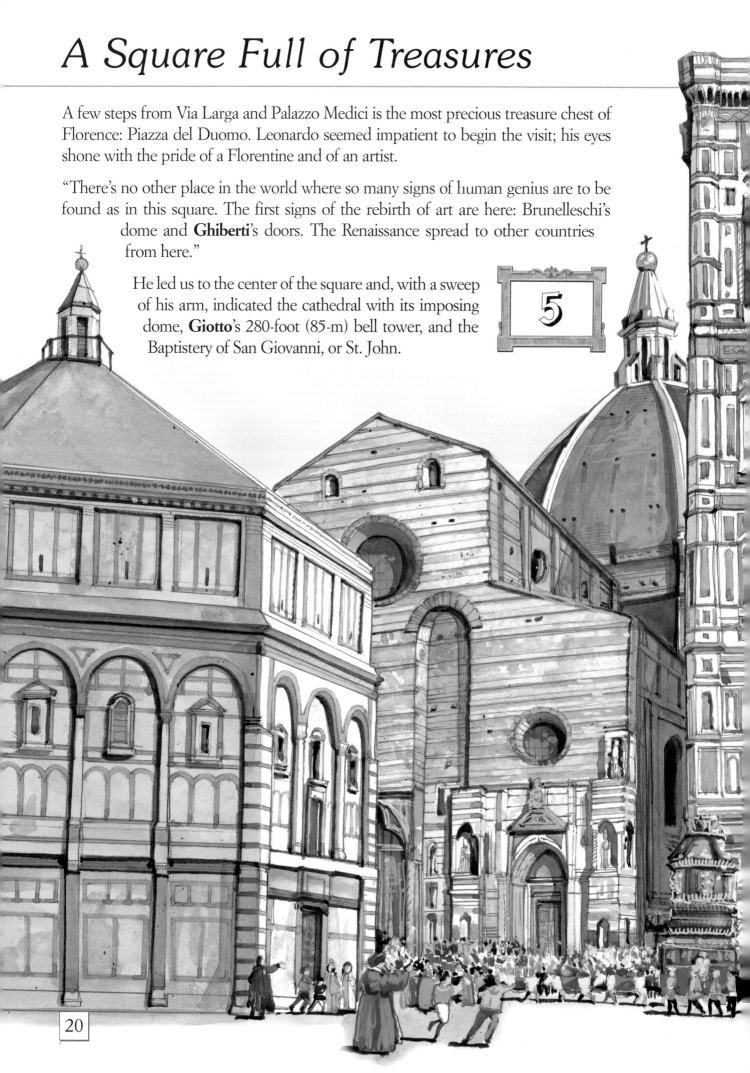

"There was an older church here once: the cathedral of Santa Reparata. Then, in 1296, the Florentines decided to build a larger and more aesthetic cathedral right on top of the old church. The new building was dedicated to Santa Maria del Fiore, or Holy Mary of the Flower. Sculptor **Arnolfo di Cambio** was the architect. Building continued under Giotto, the famous painter who had also designed the bell tower, called a *campanile* in Italian. Don't forget that artists were often painters, architects, sculptors, and engineers—sort of like myself! Various other masters worked on the cathedral, which was finally finished in 1436. The enormous dome was designed in 1402."

"Brunelleschi's dome!" Andy said, as if he knew all about it. "It's become the symbol of Florence, and is known throughout the world."

"Quite true," Leonardo agreed. "Master Brunelleschi's design was particularly daring, with a double dome where the inner one supports the framework of the outer one. There was a competition for the design—a very fair way of finding the best solution."

"The guidebook says," Andy was reading, "that it has a span of 138 feet (42 m) and is about 20 feet (6 m) higher than the bell tower."

"And the façade?" I asked, wondering why more than half of it was bare.

"It was begun by Arnolfo but, like many other Florentine churches, was never finished. The money ran out and the façade's decoration was left to be completed at some other time."

"But if that eight-sided building is the baptistery," I observed, "why is it so big?"

"San Giovanni is the oldest monument in Florence," Leonardo explained, "and there was once a Roman temple here. It's eight-sided because the number eight symbolizes a new beginning, and it's so big because baptisms took place only twice a year, so a lot of parents, godparents, and relatives had to fit inside."

"I remember hearing about the doors, too," said Andy.

"That's another treasure of this square. They are in panels of gilded bronze. Michelangelo called the doors on the east side, right across from the façade of the cathedral, the Gates of Paradise."

THE BAPTISTERY DOORS

In 1401 Lorenzo Ghiberti was commissioned to create the north doors of the baptistery. He engraved twenty-eight bronze panels with scenes from the life of Jesus Christ. Twenty years later Ghiberti made the ten panels on the east baptistery door, which illustrate scenes from the Old Testament. Michelangelo called Ghiberti's doors the Gates of Paradise.

Below: A panel from the Gates of Paradise

21

At the Old Market

After a short walk we were in the midst of a noisy, chaotic market. Good-bye to the calmness of the cathedral square. Everyone seemed to be shouting and it was hard to figure out what was going on. Fruit and vegetable venders had their crops displayed on stalls on the street; meat and fish were on tables outside the shops.

"The vegetables arrive every morning directly from the country or the city vegetable gardens," said Leonardo. "Meat and fish are strictly controlled by city police to guarantee their quality and freshness."

"I guess you can see what goes on the Florentine tables every day," Andy observed.

"Not really. Everybody can afford vegetables, but meat is only for the wealthy. The poorer people eat fish, either fresh or salted."

I was surprised to see a barber, in the midst of this food market, running his business in the open.

Leonardo explained, "Those who come from the country visit the barber not just for a shave or haircut. The barber also burns off warts, removes calluses, pulls teeth, and performs **bloodletting**."

In the meanwhile, a ruddy young man was wheeling a cart with barrels from which he drew jugs of wine.

"The tavern keepers have their wheeled stalls at the market, too," laughed Leonardo, "and you can be sure the wine they sell here is first class. That crafty host uses it to get customers to go to his tavern, where tonight he'll serve them the dregs from the barrel.

PIAZZA DELLA REPUBBLICA

The square of the old market (the forum during Roman times) and the streets around it became the Jewish **ghetto** at the end of the sixteenth century. Then, around 1890, the whole quarter was torn down to make room for the Piazza della Repubblica. Today it is the center of city life in Florence and is rimmed with cafes and shops.

A Banker's Office

"Let's get out of here," said Leonardo. "There's such a hubbub I can't even think straight. I want to show you where the real wealth of Florence comes from: the solid wealth, acquired discretely and unobtrusively."

He led us along a side street to an old palazzo, dignified but not ostentatious, and we followed him into a courtyard up to a large hall where there was practically no furniture except for a couple of desks, a few closets full of folders and papers, and a big chest with solid locks.

"Is this an office?" I whispered because it was so quiet there.

"This is a bank," Leonardo explained, "which lends money, at an interest of course, and invests money for its clients, particularly the international banking operations. So if the glory of Florence has spread throughout the world thanks to the genius of its writers and artists, its economic power has long been based on its entrepreneurs and bankers. In fact, it was here that double-entry bookkeeping was invented."

He stopped for a minute as if he were mentally calculating and then continued, "Up until fifty years ago Florence had thirty-three great banking companies with branches all over Europe. The most famous one was that of the Medici, which lent money to kings and popes. Now there are barely twenty and they have a hard time competing with German and Flemish bankers. The main banks are investment banks, but then there are also smaller money changers where you can exchange gold and silver coins from other cities and countries. Each city has its own coinage."

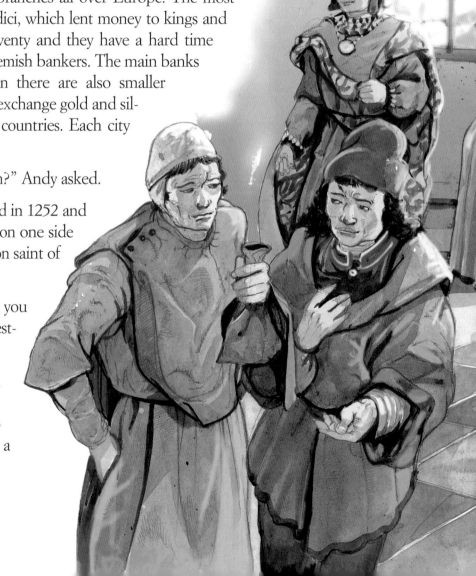

"And what is the Florentine coin?" Andy asked.

"The gold florin. It was instituted in 1252 and has the lily, symbol of Florence, on one side and Saint John the Baptist, patron saint of the city, on the other."

"And how many florins have you stowed away in international investments?" I said, jokingly.

"Even though my father was a notary, I'm awful when it comes to money," answered Leonardo with a desolate air, "I may be a genius, but not a financial one."

7

For the Glory of a Merchant

"Come on you two," Leonardo exclaimed when we were back outside. "I bet you'll like our next stop."

He led us to another square with a large dark green-and-white church. Its marble façade was finished, and a group of men were shooting their crossbows at practice targets and straw puppets.

"Oh boy!" Andy exclaimed excitedly. "I've never seen real crossbows. This is cool!"

For a moment Leonardo seemed taken aback, but then he burst out laughing. "Actually I was referring to the façade of Santa Maria Novella, but I realize that weapons and war games are more interesting to a boy your age."

"Of course, the façade too," Andy corrected himself. "It really is something!"

Leonardo winked at me and assumed the air of a teacher about to give a lecture. "Well, my young friend, this was the first of the great Florentine churches. It was begun by the Dominican friars, a **mendicant** order, in 1279. The bottom part, with niches that held sarcophagi, was already done when Giovanni Rucellai, a magistrate and wealthy wool merchant, asked the great architect **Leon Battista Alberti** to complete the façade. Ratio and proportions were what mattered. If you look carefully you'll see that the top part is a square the same size as the bottom parts on either side of the entrance. Rucellai had his emblem, the snail, worked into the decorative **frieze**. That way everyone would know who sponsored the church."

"It looks like it's closed now," said Andy. "Where do we go now?"

"I don't know about you," answered Leonardo, laughing quietly, "but I like these competitions. I think I'll stay and watch this target practice for a while."

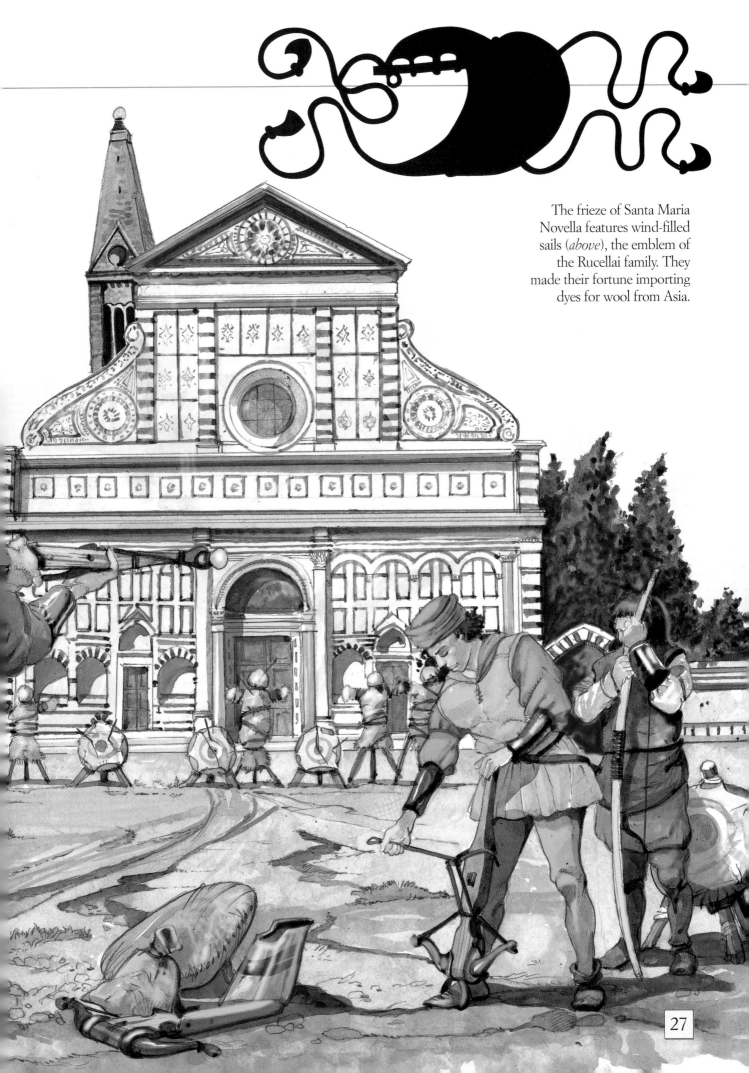

The frieze of Santa Maria Novella features wind-filled sails (*above*), the emblem of the Rucellai family. They made their fortune importing dyes for wool from Asia.

Street Life

"Florentines spend more time outside than inside; the street is like their living room. When the weather is nice they come here to talk, do business, play chess or dice, make music, and sometimes even to pray."

Leonardo explained the everyday life of the working-class citizens of Florence as we were walking along a lane that led to a *trebbio*, an intersection of three roads. At the center was a stone cross with some wax candles and a couple of oil lamps at the base.

"At night," said Leonardo, "candles and lamps at crosses and shrines are the only illumination in the deserted streets. People don't ever go out alone after dark."

While we were there, however, the sun was shining and there were a lot of people. A few women were sitting on stools and chatting as they did chores: one was mending a jacket, another was plucking a goose, and still another was preparing fruit to make jam. A tavern owner was standing at the door of his tavern. He smiled and invited us in, and even though Leonardo politely refused, the two men chatted amiably for a moment.

"Everyone is so friendly," observed Andy. "I hardly know the people who live on my floor, even though we always say hello to each other."

"Here it's like one big family," explained Leonardo. "They go to mass together in the same church, the women take their bread to the same oven to have it baked, and the men go to the same public bath."

"A public bath?" I exclaimed, rather surprised.

"They don't have running water in the houses and there are several baths in the city."

"Did you know that tavern keeper?" I asked

"No, my dear, he was just being polite. In Florence everybody calls you by your name, and often by your nickname. My first master, Andrea di Cione, was Verrocchio to everybody. The physicians and the artists have the right to be called 'maestro' by their pupils. But in general it's equality for all. Florence is a city where the social hierarchies are not all that important."

The Artist's Workshop

"You can't imagine how happy I am to show you this place. Here we are in one of the glorious Florentine art workshops, which have produced many famous artists and are training the next generation of great of artists," Leonardo explained, his eyes shining.

We were in a large room on the ground floor where a number of people, mostly young and male, were working under the guidance of an older man who went from one to another. Some were drawing or painting, some were carving or modeling with clay, and some were carrying canvases and other materials. Two boys about my age were grinding and mixing colors in a marble mortar; their hair and clothes were spotted with paint. They looked as if they were having a great time.

"I was an apprentice in a workshop like this one," Leonardo continued. "Then I got my start as artist under the guidance of Verrocchio. Among the things we studied were perspective and anatomy, because we wanted to know how the human body worked."

"But how did you become a genius?" asked Andy.

"I studied, dear boy, I studied a lot, beginning with basics. Actually, the first job Verrocchio gave me was to clean the floor, which I

remember was much dirtier than this one. Verrocchio was very strict and saw to our professional and cultural training, but he had to manage his business, too."

"You mean an art studio is a real business?" I asked, surprised.

"The Florentine workshop, my dear, is a business that produces and deals in art of all kinds, depending on what the customers ask for. Panel paintings, altarpieces, or frescoes for churches, bronze sculpture, goldwork—you name it. Workshops also design processional banners, furniture, coats of arms, and even decorations for candles and playing cards."

A Unique Sight

"Let's take a break and visit a good friend of mine," said Leonardo when we left the workshop. "His house will give you an idea of how a middle-class family lives. He'll be happy to see us."

We went up to the first floor where a servant led us into a long room with several windows. It didn't have much in the way of furniture—a rectangular table, a few high-backed chairs, a stool or two, and a painted chest. I glanced into some of the other rooms we passed: one had a wardrobe and a tabernacle with doors, another had a canopied bed

and a kneeler for prayer, and a third was full of hay-stuffed mattresses for the servants and children.

When we entered the room, there were a lot more people than I had expected—Leonardo explained that the servants and household help were also considered family. Everyone was crowded around the windows, talking excitedly.

"What's up, maestro?" Andy and I asked confused and a bit worried.

"Look for yourselves! You'll never see anything like this again!"

Framed in the window was the marble head of a young man. The statue was slowly moving by while everyone leaned out and tried to touch it. His large, unblinking eyes stared right into the room.

"I can't believe it!" gasped Andy. "Is it what I think it is?"

"Yes, my friend," Leonardo answered. "Michelangelo's young giant, his statue of David, is being hauled to its place next to the Palazzo della Signoria. It will be the symbol of republican freedom against tyranny. Let's go down to the square. I don't want to miss this!"

Setting up David

When we got to Piazza della Signoria, the colossal statue of David, still in its wooden scaffolding, had been set in front of Palazzo Vecchio while the crowd watched and cheered. It had taken forty men four days to move it here, sliding it on greased wooden

Right: The Marzocco lion was a heraldic symbol of justice and protector of the Roman Republic. Donatello sculpted a life-sized lion in 1419 for the platform of Palazzo della Signoria (today Palazzo Vecchio). The one show here is a 6-foot (2-m) weather-vane that was placed on top of the tower (*left*).

cylinders from the work yard of the Opera del Duomo, where Michelangelo had sculpted it. The beautiful white marble stood out against the dark stone wall of the building.

"Everyone knows that Michelangelo and I have never seen eye to eye," admitted Leonardo, "but I recognize the greatness of this statue—it will be eternal."

"It sounds as if you're a bit envious, maestro," said Andy brazenly. "But the world—my world—thinks of you both as geniuses."

Leonardo nodded thoughtfully, then began speaking: "This square is the heart of Florentine political life. Citizens meet here in public assembly when the big bell on Palazzo della Signoria—the government building—is rung. Speakers address the crowd from that platform along the façade. The building itself was designed by Arnolfo di Cambio in 1299, after designing the Duomo, and finished in 1322. It's built like a fortress and, as a symbol of authority, its tower is higher than all the other towers in Florence."

"It is a real fortress," observed Andy, "and must have an interesting history."

"I'm sure you'll see the inside tomorrow," noted Leonardo. "Architects and artists were always adding things, like the courtyard by Michelozzo—the architect who built the Medici palace in Via Larga—that was added over fifty years later."

"And the *loggia* over to the right?" I asked, "What's that used for?"

"The town council decided they needed a *loggia* in 1374 and had one designed by **Andrea Orcagna**. It's used for public ceremonies and the magistrates meet here to handle the affairs of state because they're protected from the weather but visible to the people. Don't forget that a government is the administrator, not the master, of the Florentine people."

"And now there's another very attentive guardian," Andy observed. "David with his slingshot will keep an eye on the *loggia* and the work of the magistrates."

The Butchers' Bridge

Leonardo's tour brought us back to the Arno River, right on the Ponte Vecchio. "Seen from the inside it looks more like a street than a bridge," said Leonardo. "It's busy like the market because all the little buildings here are shops. Most of them are butcher shops and tanneries, but there are also blacksmiths and fish sellers, and they all throw their garbage into the Arno. The bridge used to belong to the state, and the rent was an important source of money for the tax office. But ten years ago it was ceded to private owners."

"It's one of the most famous bridges in the world," said Andy. "When was the first version built?"

"The first bridge was wooden and built when Florence was a Roman colony," Leonardo explained. "In 1080, I believe, it was replaced by a stone bridge that collapsed one hundred years later. The Florentines rebuilt it immediately, but the Arno has a mind of its own: in summer the river is almost dry, but then it swells with the winter rains and becomes threatening. In 1333 a flood destroyed the bridge again. The bridge you see now was built in 1345; architects incorporated two strong piers with prow-shaped buttresses for support."

From a low stone railing we watched the boats pass below, laden with barrels of wine, bales of wool, lumber, construction stones, or salt. The Arno, Leonardo explained, was navigable up to its mouth. Barges and rafts could go down the river, but it was difficult to sail against the current to Pisa.

The water looked so calm, but the noise around us was deafening: venders shouting, horses and wagons passing by, people arguing.

"There's too much confusion in this city," Leonardo sighed. "I need some peace and quiet. Let's go outside the walls and visit one of the many country estates. Most wealthy Florentines have a villa or farm in the country, in addition to the houses where they live and the workshops where they work. Cafaggiolo, where the Medici family has an estate, is not far away and is particularly relaxing."

JEWELS ON DISPLAY

In 1593 Ferdinand I, the grand duke of Tuscany, was bothered by the noise and odor of the shops of tanners, butchers, and fishmongers. He ordered the shops be given to goldsmiths and jewelers. Since then display windows along Ponte Vecchio have been filled with jewelry, both antique and modern. It is a popular place to buy jewelry for both locals and tourists.

A Villa in the Country

"The villa of Cafaggiolo was once an old castle. The Medicis turned it into a peaceful country residence where wheat, wine, and oil are produced. They have all they need and what's left over is sold. Friends often hunt and fish when they visit."

"I'm against hunting," I said decidedly, "but I do like dogs and horses."

"This is a hunt with a falcon, which used to be a sport only for lords. When the falconer takes the hood off the bird, sweeps up his arm, and gives a sharp order, the bird flies up and looks for prey. The hunters follow on horseback, guided by the bell the falcon has on one leg, and the pack of dogs—greyhounds, basset hounds, and bloodhounds—find the prey and recover it."

Andy and I played with the dogs for a while but kept our distance from the falcon.

THE MEDICI VILLAS

The Medici family was particularly active in building and decorating villas and country properties. In addition to Cafaggiolo, which had been in the Medici family for generations, Cosimo de' Medici and his heirs purchased and renovated country residences across the Tuscany region.

Farewell at Porta San Frediano

When we returned to Florence we snacked on bread, cheese, and some marvelous olives we got in Cafaggiolo.

"My dear friends," said Leonardo, "you came into my world by crossing a bridge and now it's time to return to yours through that gate." He gestured across the square.

"You mean the visit is over, maestro?" I asked, feeling disappointed. "But there are still so many other things to see!"

"You'll do that tomorrow, with your friends and your guide. But you'll be the only ones who know what life in Florence was like during its most splendid period."

"Isn't there something else you can tell us? This gate, for example …"

"You never give up, do you Frannie? So you want to know something about the gate. Well, this is Leonardo's last lesson. Porta San Frediano is one of the fifteen gates within the city's walls, which were built in 1333. People traveling to Pisa leave through this gate. Those heavy oak doors are closed at night. Next to them are the benches of the tax collectors because everything that goes out and comes into the city is taxed."

"I hope we don't have to buy a ticket to leave!" said Andy, laughing. "Good-bye maestro, and thank you so much for everything."

"Farewell, children, I'm honored to have been of service to you."

The Renaissance in Florence

Florence was in turmoil in early 1401, but it had nothing to do with politics. There was a competition to design the north doors of the baptistery, the venerable building that stood across from the cathedral. The carved doors had been ordered by the powerful corporation, or guild, of the wool merchants, who wanted to show their high civic sense by enriching one of the most prestigious buildings in the city.

A competition, then! May the best win. But was the winner really the best? It is hard to say who was best with artists like Lorenzo Ghiberti, Filippo Brunelleschi, and Jacopo della Quercia, who was the oldest of the three men at twenty-seven. Lorenzo's elegant designs won, and the door was his. In retrospect, it seems that the jury overlooked, and perhaps didn't recognize, the innovative elements in Brunelleschi's trial panel, which heralded a new vision of art and man: the seed of the early Renaissance had been sown. Filippo did not know that he would later win the commission to build the dome for Santa Maria del Fiore cathedral, more commonly called the Duomo, which means "dome" in Italian.

The two artists each had enthusiastic admirers and riotous detractors, nothing new for Florence. Despite their unified pride in the city, Florentines were very competitive and when a guild, a family, or an association sponsored a monument, the goal was often to outdo the splendor of those its rival had built. In the wealthy patrician class, which had always been divided into factions, rivalries sometimes became violent and lasted for generations. The power and influence of the great families was measured by the number of their followers, who often lived around the principal residence of the family they supported.

Left: A portrait of Lorenzo the Magnificent by Giorgio Vasari.

Below: The watercolor *Carta della Catena* gives a bird's-eye view of Florence in 1480.

In the fifteenth century the most powerful family in the city was the Medicis. The first great member was Cosimo the Elder (1389–1464), a banker who was more powerful than a prince. Entrepreneur, statesman, and patron of the arts, Cosimo governed the state from his palazzo in Via Larga, although he left the old republican institutions intact. His grandson Lorenzo, known as the Magnificent (1449–1492), also a patron of all the arts and man of learning, accepted the leadership of the state but modified the city statutes to reinforce his own rule, marking the cultural and artistic zenith of Florence. He also created a balance among the Italian city-states that lasted until after his death.

After Lorenzo, the times changed. The Medici were banished from the city in 1494 and Florence fell under the sway of the Dominican friar Savonarola (1452–1498), who railed against luxury, the degeneration of customs, and ecclesiastic corruption from the San Marco convent. Savonarola put himself at the head of a Christian republic and burned books, paintings, and treasures he considered superfluous and dangerous, an event known as the Bonfire of the Vanities. Not even his tragic death—he was hanged and then burned as a heretic on orders of Pope Alexander VI—could atone for his actions. Savonarola was an ambiguous man that some believe is a saint. Others consider him a madman, martyr, and terrorist.

After Savonarola the Republic, under the guidance of Pier Soderini (1453–1522), was short lived. In 1512 Cardinal Giovanni de' Medici, son of Lorenzo the Magnificent, triumphantly returned to Florence and became pope—Leo X—the following year.

Chronology

59 BCE – Julius Caesar's legionaries found the Florentine colony during the spring festivals dedicated to the goddess Flora, which is probably the source of the name *Florentia*, later changed to Florence (Firenze).

ca. 30 BCE – The first circle of city walls is built.

451 CE – After being attacked by King Totila's Goths, the Florentines build a second circle of walls.

570 – Beginning of the Lombard dominion.

786 – Charlemagne drives the Lombards from Florence and installs a Frankish count.

ca. 800 – The third circle of walls is built as defense against the Hungars.

1076–1115 – Matilda of Canossa becomes Countess of Tuscany and has the fourth circle of walls is built.

1138 – Florence becomes a commune (free city) and elects two consuls.

1175 – The fifth circle of city walls is built.

1193 – Constitution of the seven guilds, or principal corporations, in Florence.

1216 – Beginning of quarrels between the Guelphs, partisans of the pope, and the Ghibellines, partisans of the emperor.

1218 – The second bridge after Ponte Vecchio is inaugurated in Florence. It is called Ponte Nuovo (new bridge), later Ponte alla Carraia.

1237 – The Milanese magistrate Rubaconte commissions a third bridge. It was initially named after him, but is now called Ponte alle Grazie.

1252 – The gold florin is minted. Construction of the bridge of Santa Trinita, the fourth in Florence.

1255 – Beginning of the construction of Palazzo del Popolo, later Bargello.

1284 – Construction of the sixth circle of city walls begins.

1293 – Giano della Bella's Ordinances of Justice decree makes guild membership a requirement for holding office.

1333 – Disastrous flood of the Arno River.

1342–1346 – Many Florentine banks close down, including the Bardi, Peruzzi, Acciaiuoli, and Bonaccorsi.

1348 – The Black Death cuts the population of Florence in half. A university is built in Florence.

1429 – Cosimo the Elder is at the head of the Medici family (and, indirectly, of the state).

1469–1492 – Lorenzo de' Medici (the Magnificent) rules.

1478 – Pazzi conspiracy: Lorenzo escapes, but his brother Giuliano is killed.

1494 – The Medici are banished from Florence.

1498 – Savonarola is put to death in Piazza della Signoria.

1529–1530 – The troops of the emperor Charles V lay siege to Florence and return the Medici to power.

1537 – Cosimo, member of a cadet branch of the Medici, is named head of Florence.

1540 – The court moves from the palace in Via Larga to Palazzo Vecchio.

1560 – Construction begins on the Uffizi under the direction of **Giorgio Vasari**.

1564 – Cosimo orders the construction of the Vasari corridor that joins Palazzo Vecchio to Palazzo Pitti, bought by his wife Eleonora of Toledo.

1569 – Cosimo is named grand duke of Tuscany by Pope Pius V.

1571–1737 – The last of the Medici succeed each other on the throne: Francesco, Ferdinando, Francesco II, Cosimo II, Ferdinando II, Cosimo III, and Gian Gastone.

1574 – The Florentine Jews are relegated to the ghetto.

1583 – Founding of the Accademia della Crusca, whose purpose is to purify the language.

1652 – Ferdinando Tacca builds the Pergola Theater.

1737 – The Medici dynasty comes to an end. Francis of Lorraine becomes grand duke of Tuscany.

1765–1859 – Grand dukes of Austrian origin reign: Peter Leopold, Ferdinand III, and Leopold II.

1801 – Napoleon founds the kingdom of Etruria.

1860 – By popular vote Tuscany becomes part of the constitutional monarchy of the kingdom of Italy.

1864 – Florence is proclaimed capital of Italy.

1865–1874 – The architect Giuseppe Poggi tears down the old city walls and gives the Florence a new urban plan.

1867 – The novelist Alessandro Manzoni (author of *The Betrothed*) proposes spoken Florentine as the national language.

1871 – Rome becomes the capital of Italy.

1873 – Michelangelo's *David* is moved from Piazza della Signoria to the Galleria dell'Accademia.

1887 – The façade of the cathedral of Florence, by architect De Fabris, is inaugurated.

1933 – Giovanni Michelucci designs the railroad station of Santa Maria Novella.

1933 – The Maggio Musicale Fiorentino, an opera festival, is founded.

1944 – The Germans blow up all the bridges over the Arno except Ponte Vecchio. The city is liberated on August 11.

1960 – Giovanni Michelucci builds the futuristic church of San Giovanni Battista.

1966 – Flood of Florence (November).

1980 – Florence celebrates the Medici with five large exhibitions.

1986 – Florence is elected the year's European capital of culture.

Glossary

Alberti, Leon Battista, (1401–1472) architect, writer, and town planner. He considered architecture as a direct recovery of the classical spirit of Rome. Among his buildings are the Tempio Malatestiano in Rimini, Palazzo Rucellai in Florence, and the church of San Sebastiano in Mantua.

Annunciation, the appearance of the angel Gabriel to the Virgin Mary telling her she would have a baby, Jesus Christ.

Black Death, the plague that killed great numbers of people, particularly in the fourteenth century.

bloodletting, a medieval practice of removing blood for medicinal purposes.

Brunelleschi, Filippo, (1377–1446) architect. He began as a goldsmith and sculptor, but became famous as an architect. In addition to the dome of Santa Maria del Fiore, the Pazzi chapel, and the Spedale degli Innocenti, he designed the churches of San Lorenzo and Santo Spirito, and Palazzo Pitti, all in Florence.

Corinthian, the most elaborate style of ancient Greek architecture. Column capitals are carved with flowers, leaves, and vines.

della Robbia, Andrea, (1435–1525) sculptor and ceramist. He was known for his polychrome ceramics.

di Cambio, Arnolfo, (1245–1308) architect and sculptor. He worked in Siena, Orvieto, Bologna, Rome, and Florence. In Florence he designed Santa Maria del Fiore, Santa Croce, and Palazzo Vecchio.

de' Medici, Lorenzo, (1449–1492) known as the Magnificent. In 1469 he inherited the *signoria* (rule) of the city of Florence from his father Pietro. He was a shrewd statesman, a great patron of the arts, and a poet.

Francis of Assisi, (1182–1226), saint, friar, and founder of the Franciscan order. Known for his love of nature and the simplicity of his way of life.

frieze, a richly ornamented part of the entablature on a building.

ghetto, part of a city where members of a minority group live, usually because of social, legal, or economic pressure.

Ghiberti, Lorenzo, (1378–1455) goldsmith, sculptor, and architect. He designed two of the bronze doors on the baptistery in Florence after winning a competition with his rival Brunelleschi. Both artists' panels, which depict the sacrifice of Isaac, are on display at the Bargello Museum in Florence.

Giotto, (1267–1337) painter, architect, and sculptor. He painted the frescoes of the legend of Saint Francis in the basilica of San Francesco in Assisi, the Scrovegni Chapel in Padua, and the Bardi Chapel in Santa Croce in Florence. He also painted panels such as the *Crucifix* and the *Ognissanti Madonna*.

guild, or corporation, a medieval association of merchants or craftsmen. The seven principal guilds in Florence were for merchants, judges and notaries, money exchangers, wool, silk, physicians and pharmacists, and furriers.

loggia, a covered gallery or entrance that is open on one side.

mendicant, a beggar.

Michelangelo Buonarroti, (1475–1564) sculptor, painter, architect, and poet. As a boy he lived at the court of Lorenzo the Magnificent, but then went to Venice, Bologna, and Rome. Among his most famous sculptures are the *Pieta*, the *David*, the *Moses*, and those at the Medici tombs at the church of San Lorenzo in Florence (Medici Chapels), where he also did the architectural project. Michelangelo is also famous for painting the ceiling of the Sistine Chapel in the Vatican. He designed the dome of Saint Peter's in Rome, which was built after his death.

Michelozzo, (1396–1472) sculptor and architect. Inspired by classical Roman architecture, he built the convent of San Marco, the Medici palace, and the Medici villas of Careggi and Cafaggiolo for Cosimo de' Medici.

Orcagna, Andrea, (ca. 1308–1368) Florentine architect, painter, and sculptor. His main work is the tabernacle of the church of Orsanmichele in Florence. The *loggia* in Piazza della Signoria has been attributed to him, but was actually designed by his brother.

Pazzi, family of bankers in Florence and rivals of the Medici, involved in the conspiracy to replace the Medici as rulers of Florence (April 26, 1478).

Vasari, Giorgio, (1511–1574) painter, architect, and writer. He worked in Rome and Florence, where he renovated and decorated Palazzo Vecchio, designed the Uffizi museum, and wrote biographies of Italian painters.

Verrocchio, (1436–1488) Andrea di Cione. A sculptor, painter, and goldsmith. He was Leonardo da Vinci's teacher. He sculpted the *Doubting Thomas* for the church of Orsanmichele in Florence and the equestrian monument of Bartolomeo Colleoni in Venice.

Index

Page numbers in **boldface** are illustrations, tables, and charts.